AM I MY SISTER'S KEEPER?

Keisha Williams

Illustrated by **Garrett Myers**

Something to Think About:

Do you ever get frustrated with your siblings or have gotten so mad that you wished something bad would happen to them? This is a problem that is common amongst most siblings. However, it is not a problem that is so unique to God. Caleb is given biblical truth which encourages him to reflect the god-like character and the attitude that he should take concerning his conflicts in regards to his sister. Read to find out will good moral character to be produced & demonstrated in Caleb's current situation.

This Book belongs to: _____

Given By: _____

Date: _____

Message:

_____
_____
_____
_____
_____
_____
_____
_____
_____

Author's Purpose:

Personal Effort to Be a Better Mother

Looking at my son Caleb, I see that, on the inside, his emotions would sometimes reflect anger and frustration. He seems to always be in trouble about something and his attitude makes it worse. The funny thing is, however, he has a big heart. Sometimes, I feel that when he is alone in his room fuming, he is thinking that we, his parents, love his sibling more than we love him, but that couldn't be further from the truth. I am frustrated that decisions he makes as the older sibling is based on something that the younger sister requests, and he carries it out knowing that it is the wrong thing to do as well as potentially dangerous: jumping on the bed, riding bikes inside the house, going outside without permission, etc. So, I would fuss or yell making things worse, although what I really want to do is help him work through problems and cause him to feel good about himself and understand the consequences concerning the decisions he makes, but my method was only exhausting me.

After some deep inner searching, an idea came to me. Why not use actual conflicts that derive in our home, put them in children story format, and match it to biblical incidents related to sibling rivalry and scriptural reference? I would then use the research to create solutions to help Caleb, Lailah and other adolescents their age develop better attitudes about life, as well as help parents who are just as frustrated. Realizing that my children are God's gift to me and my husband, it is very important that we are careful to nurture them in His light. The Bible says to train up a child in the way that he should go and when he is old, he will not depart from it. It is never too early to teach our children about **love** and **respect** for each other. **Love** begins at home. Something is wrong if they treat friends outside of the home better than those inside of the home. We should automatically teach our children manners, how to be polite to adults, things not to do or say in public....but how well do we reinforce this inside of the home? Do we overlook it hoping that it will get better as they get older? We must encourage the right practices now, but unfortunately, children didn't come with manuals. So, we have to use trial and error. I believe, since we as parents are all in this together, and it does take a village to raise a child, why not use my real trials to create beautiful stories to reach our children. Children learn differently also. Some only need to hear it and they understand. I think others are like Caleb and Lailah, visual, the picture is clearer when they are given the opportunity to see it. Then, they understand. So, allow me to use our stories as teachable moments.

In Loving Memory of my father...Apostle Colonel James Thomas

Caleb is seven years old. He is so frustrated. "Why does Lailah always get her way?" he thinks to himself, "It's not fair!" Lailah is Caleb's younger sister. She is four years old. Caleb frowns as he watches his sister throw her arms around mommy and plants a great big kiss on her cheek.

He rolls his eyes, goes to his room, plops down on the floor, and folds his arms across his chest letting out a deep sigh. "That was some performance, she knows she knocked down all those tapes, but mommy fusses at me and makes me pick them up!" He thinks to himself. Enraged even more, he blurts out, "I hate her, I wish I didn't have a sister . . .." Standing outside of his bedroom, mother and father hear their son and are saddened.

The next morning, Caleb jumps out of bed and as usual rushes to his sister's room to wake her up to go play. He forgets that he was still mad at her about the tapes she knocked down last night. As he turns the corner, he begins to call her name, "Lailah wake up!"

He turns the doorknob and opens her door. When he looks inside, he's shocked by what he sees. His little sister is not in her bed. In fact, there is no bed in her room at all.

In her room are a big brown desk, computers, telephone, and big bookshelf with so many books!

He rushes to his parent's bedroom, "Mama…Daddy wake up…Lailah is Gone! Where is she?"

Groggily, Dad turns over squinting to open his eyes. Mama yawns a great big yawn, "What's the matter Caleb? What's with all the noise so early in the morning?"

"Someone took all of Lailah's things out of her room and she's nowhere to be found! Her bed, teddy bears, dolls, clothes…." He gushes out the words sadly.

"Wait, wait wait one minute Caleb, who took what from where? Who is Lailah? What are you talking about?

"Daddy, Lailah my sister, you know Lailah! She is gone! Come look in her room!" he grabs dad's hands and rushes to the room. Inside, he was hoping it was all a dream and that all of her things would be there when they arrived.

However, it was no dream at all, Lailah was indeed not there.

"Caleb, I think you had a bad dream. It's just my office. You don't have a sister named Lailah." Caleb's eyes grow big and he is really frightened because he knows that he has a sister, or does he?

Of course, there has to be a Lailah! She was just here last night playing with him. Was it a dream?

"No daddy! Why are you saying that? You know I have a sister and her name is Lailah! She lives with us, we got her from the hospital, and she's four years old! Wait, I'll show you in the living room!"

He runs to the living room to find pictures of her on the tables, mantle and walls. Caleb is now in the living room frantically searching the walls and running from table to table and finally stops in front of the mantelpiece.

All of the pictures are of him!

Also, pictures of Caleb and his mom and dad! What is going on? Where is Lailah? Caleb could hear mama in the kitchen preparing breakfast. Dad had gone into the bathroom to shave and prepare for the day.

It was a beautiful Saturday and there was no school today. Caleb slowly went back to his room and sat down on the floor.

It didn't make sense. He knew he had had a sister at one time or another, and every Saturday they would watch cartoons and see just how much trouble they could get into before mom would fuss. Could it have all been a dream? No, there has to be a sister!

He began to try to remember everything and anything about Lailah that would help him convince his parents that she was real.

First thing, he thought to himself, "I have to remember the very last time we were together." He closed his eyes, still sprawled out on the floor, and there she was laughing and skipping around the den. "Come on Caleb! Betcha can't catch me. Act like a bear and say Grrrrrr!"

She continued to laugh and play. Caleb saw himself too playing along with her, running around the table acting like a bear and enjoying the role-play. Then he saw her turn around to see how close he was to catching her and that's when it happened.

All over the floor the collection of tapes went. Lailah had forgotten that their collection of tapes was near the T.V., and as she tried to escape the bear ran right into it. There was such a terrible noise. The noise frightened Lailah that she ran over to Caleb.

At that moment, mom came into the room. He remembered getting angry for having to pick up the tapes. He remembered going to his room, plopping down on the floor and . . .

Caleb sat up straight, frozen, as if he had seen a ghost. "It's all my fault! I had forgotten about the tapes, frantically he jumps to his feet."

"Mom, Dad!" He ran to the kitchen just as his mother was getting ready to call him to breakfast. Dad was already seated and waiting for them to join the table.

"I have something to tell you. I know what happened to Lailah! It's all my fault! It's all my fault!" Tears began to well up and he was breathing as if he had just run a marathon.

"Calm down Caleb" Mother began to hug him close. Dad stood up and walked over to where his son was standing.

"Son, what are you talking about? It's alright . . ."
"No daddy, It's all my fault that Lailah is not here." He started to cry.
"Lailah?" His parents exchanged expressions. "Who is Lailah?"
"My sister!" Now he was frustrated. How could they forget? "Your daughter, and I was so mad at her and now she's gone!"
"Well . . ." He began to tell them about the tapes in the den, pretending to be a bear, his sister knocking over the tapes, and his mom making him clean up the mess.

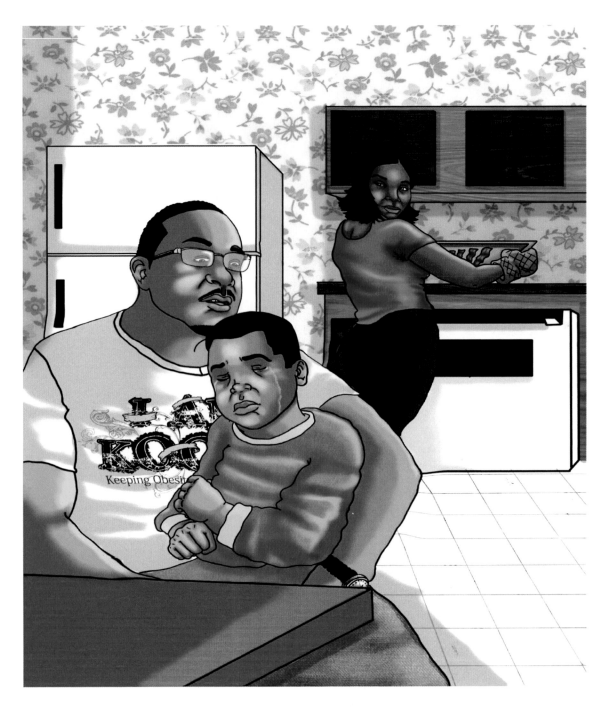

" I was so mad that I went to my room and wished her away. I didn't mean it, I promise! I never meant to wish her away. I'm sorry. I'm so sorry." Tears trickled down his face as he buried his face into his dad's chest.

His father sighed as though he was in deep thought. "You know son, we have to be careful of things we say and do concerning each other.

Did you know that our words have power? If we speak things with a certain level of belief, then those things that we say either positive or negative can come to life."

"Really?" Caleb looked up at his father intently.

"Yes, as a matter of fact, it reminds me of a story of two brothers who lived a long time age. One was a farmer, and the other tended sheep. They both loved what they did and chose to offer a sacrifice to God.

God accepted only one brother's gift but did not receive the other because he did not give from a genuine heart. This brother became so angry that he began to hate his brother. One day, his anger and jealousy grew so that he hurt his brother, and his brother went away forever.

God was unhappy because of the harm that was done to his poor brother. So, God punished him and sent him away never to see his parents again. His parents were so sad because in one day they had lost two sons.

"Wow" Caleb listened closely, "that is sad." Then it dawned on him. "Dad, I wished my sister away and that wasn't good. Will God send me away too?"

"I don't think so Caleb, but I'm sure he wants you to understand how hurtful and serious words like those can be. He wants us to love each other. Do you know what the brother asked him?"

"No, what?"

"Am I my brother's keeper? The answer to that is yes you are. So, son, if you feel responsible for hurting someone, it's your responsibility to make it right."

"How do I do that?" He asked.

"Well son, I can't tell you what to do, but I am sure that if you search deep within your heart, the answer will come to you and you will do the right thing."

"Dad, I'm not really hungry. Can I be excused?"

"Go ahead son."

Caleb hugged his dad, slid down from his lap and headed towards his room. Standing in his doorway he paused to look at the door that he remembered that use to read "Lailah's Things".

He sighed as he went on into his room and sat down in his favorite spot. There on his rug that displayed trains of all shapes and sizes, he fell into deep thought.

"What would be the right thing to do?"

Then, it hit him, he would talk to God.

"God, I really did a horrible thing. I said something about my sister and wished her away. I didn't mean it. Now I know that my words have power, and I want to use my words to make it right again. Please bring my sister back. I really do miss her. I promise to never use words that would hurt her or anyone else. I love my sister and as her big brother, it is my job to look after her. I am my sister's keeper. I was wrong for getting so mad, and I just want to tell her that I'm sorry. Could please help me Lord?"

Closing his eyes he felt a sense of peace come over him and he began to feel happy again.

Then, he heard the doorbell ring. Voices entered that sounded oh so familiar. There was a real familiar voice that made him jump to his feet and rush downstairs. Running as though his life depended on it, he charged into the den. Abruptly, he stopped at the doorway and his face lit up.

"Caleb!" She said as she ran into him almost knocking him over. She was real!

At first, he was almost too stunned to move. Then, he threw his arms around her as tears rolled down his little cheeks.

"Lailah, I miss you so much, and I'm sorry that I got so mad at you."

"It's okay Caleb, we all make mistakes." His parents simply smiled at each other. Grandpa cleared his throat.

"Grandma, Grandpa!" He said as he hugged them. "Lailah was with you the whole time?"

"Why yes! We took her with us while your mom and dad had her room renovated. They didn't tell you? Grandma looked at dad a bit confused.

"Well, we didn't quite get around to it. Something came up" Dad smiled and winked at his son.

"Dad, why is your office in Lailah's room?" Now he wanted some answers.

"Well, because she took my office, which is much bigger.
Did you look in my office?"

Located downstairs, he ran to his dad's office and immediately spotted the sign that read "Lailah's Things".

He opened the door wide and all of her furniture was inside from the dresser, bed and dolls. He turned around relieved and turned to his parents, Lailah and Grandparents who had followed him into the room.

"Well, I have one thing to say. The next time, I need to know where she is because I AM MY SISTER'S KEEPER!"

They all laughed together as he gave his sister the biggest hug ever.

Discussion Questions for Parents and Children:

Who is the main character?

What is the name of Caleb's sister?

Where does the story does takes place?

Why is Caleb so angry in the beginning of the story?

Do you feel Caleb has a good reason to be angry? Why or Why not?

What happens to make Caleb have a change of heart?

Caleb's dad tells him a story about two brothers. What lesson was his dad trying to teach him with this story?

Have you ever been angry at your brother or sister and said something that you did not mean?

Do you feel words can be harmful?

   If you had to help Caleb with his problem, what would have been your solution to the problem?

Are you your brother's or sister's keeper? How?

Caleb & Lailah Williams!

"We Love Each Other….We Really Do!"

About the Author:

Mrs. Keisha Williams is a pastor's daughter, wife, mother and a teacher whose background consists of extensive training in Education. She has received certifications in Early Childhood Education, Middle Grades, ESOL and Spanish. She has been teaching for 15 years. Mrs. Williams strives to teach new concepts in a variety of ways so that all students, depending on their individual needs, can learn and reach their full potential.

Mrs. Williams is very involved in her school and community. Mrs. Williams and her husband also established a non-profit, Keeping Obesity Out of Life's Loop (K.O.O.L.L.) program, and has served both communities and schools by offering a variety of programs to promote health. Their program also targets Anti-Bullying and focuses on building positive character. She has assisted with many programs at her school and for her efforts to help students become healthy, using the Atlanta's First Down for Fitness program, she was chosen by the Atlanta Falcons as one of their 2012-2013 Teachers of the Year. In 2013-2014 she was also named Teacher of the Year for her school as well.

Mrs. K. Williams, affectionately called by her students, currently leads an organization of high school young ladies called G.I.F.T.S. or Girls in Focus to Succeed. She inspires these young women to achieve high GPA's, be active in their communities, empower each other, build self-confidence and know their worth.

Mrs. Williams believes that children should know that Knowledge is power and the instruction they are receiving will enable them to better every aspect of their lives and give them an opportunity for a successful future.

Garrett resides in Albany, Georgia. He has been drawing since he was a little boy. He is gifted and talented and uses his gifts and talents to glorify God in all that he draws. He always reminds others that his drawings are creations from God, and his tools are His handiworks.

Made in United States
Orlando, FL
04 October 2023

37496001R00020